HOW TO
REARRANGE
THE WORLD

Other books by Todd Temple

How to Become a Teenage Millionaire

Creative Dating
(with Doug Fields)

52 Simple Ways to Teach Your Child About God

52 Ways to Show Aging Parents You Care
(with Tracy Green)

HOW TO REARRANGE THE WORLD*

TODD TEMPLE

OLIVER
NELSON

THOMAS NELSON PUBLISHERS
NASHVILLE

Published in Nashville, Tennessee, by Oliver-Nelson Books, a division of Thomas Nelson, Inc., Publishers, and distributed in Canada by Lawson Falle, Ltd., Cambridge, Ontario.

The Bible version used in this publication is THE NEW KING JAMES VERSION. Copyright © 1979, 1980, 1982, Thomas Nelson, Inc., Publishers.

Printed in the United States.

**Library of Congress
Cataloging-in-Publication Data**

Temple, Todd, 1958–
    How to rearrange the world / Todd Temple.
        p.   c.m.
     ISBN 0-8407-9593-9
     1. Teenagers—Conduct of life. 2. Social change. I. Title.
    BJ1661.T44   1992
    170'.835—dc20   92–3710
                          CIP

CONTENTS

START HERE

First

Lots of great books are filled with practical ways to clean up the environment, help the homeless, save hungry people, and improve your community. Several of them have even made the best-seller lists. I bet you have one or two of them on your bookshelf. If there are so many good "you can make a difference" books available, why would I want to write another?

Because changing the world requires more than just going out and doing good things. Getting involved with the latest social concern fad will make a difference only till the next cool cause makes headlines, cover stories, and benefit concerts—and the country turns from feeding starving people to recycling plastic.

To make a real and *lasting* difference on this planet, we need more than "cause groupies"—we need world changers.

This book shows you how to become a world changer. Each chapter reveals a quality you're likely to find in the lives of people who've made the biggest positive impact on our world. Whether your concern is hunger or homelessness, AIDS or alcoholism, racism or recycling—or all of these—each chapter can help you develop habits and attitudes that can make a difference.

Think of it as a training camp. I'll show you new ways of thinking and acting and then let you practice what you've learned. Each chapter ends with a week's worth of suggestions so that you can try out the idea.

Second

The Appendix contains some ideas for getting involved in change. There are many areas of need in our world, all of them desperate for people who can make a difference. But I don't want to overwhelm you with the world's problems and all the things you should do to fix them, so I chose to talk about just four: AIDS, disasters, the environment, and homeless people. I picked these needs because they're ones in which students can make a great difference right now.

Third

One last thing. I just wanted to tell you why I wrote this book to students rather than to the general adult audience. I did it for one reason: you're the ones who will make the greatest difference. It's sad, but most adults are so stuck in their habits and attitudes that if they aren't already world changers at heart, they never will be.

It's different with you. You're still shaping your view of the world and your place in it. Your values, attitudes, people skills, money habits, and priorities are still being formed. While you're open to change, I want to expose you to a life-style that doesn't get a lot of airplay in our society. (If it did, I think the world wouldn't be in such an awful spot.)

You're not just the hope of our future. You're our hope *now*. You can make this world different—but only if you're willing to *be* different.

Todd Temple
Del Mar, California

1
Dream Big

This is an active book. Sometimes I'm going to ask you to get up and do something. Like now. Lie down on the floor and stare up at the ceiling. If you're reading this on a subway or in class, I'm sorry—do it anyway. (If someone asks you what you're doing, just show this authorization.)

Are you on your back looking up? Okay, now imagine this situation. For some strange reason, the building you're in has been turned completely upside down—you're somehow suspended from what *used to be* the floor, looking down on what *used to be* the ceiling. While you're hanging there, think about these questions:

- If you fell to the "ceiling," what would you hit? If it's sloped, will you slide to the "peak"? What else will fall with you?
- Can you rearrange the room to work upside down? Will you need to rehang the curtains? Get longer lamp cords? Will you be able to reach the light switches? Will you have to duck through the doorway or climb through it?
- Will you still vacuum the carpet? Will your parents tell you to pick up your floor? If you walk barefoot, will you get "cottage cheese" between your toes?
- If the bathroom used to be the second door on the left, where is it now? If the toilet paper was hung to fall off the top, how is it hung now? Does the faucet work? How about the toilet?

End of experiment: you may get off the floor now (but if you're comfortable, you're welcome to stay there). You just did an amazing thing. You turned a building upside down *in your mind*. You created something in your imagination that doesn't exist in reality. Although the building has never been upside down, you've seen it that way—and you have mental pictures to prove it.

In other words, you asked yourself *what if?*, and your imagination answered.

What if? is an important question. If reality—**what is**—is the best it can be, there's little point in asking *what if?*; you couldn't possibly imagine something better. But that certainly isn't the case.

Our world is far from perfect. You can imagine one that's better and even entertain the thought of trying to get there. You can ask *what if?*

There's another word for *what-if*ing: dreaming.

World Changers Are Dreamers

Imagine that you and your friends are tired of **what is,** fed up with the government's unfair taxes, oppression, neglect. You're tired of the way it controls and restricts religion, the press, and free enterprise. So you get together and start asking *what if? What if* we formed our *own* nation? What would it look like? What freedoms would we protect? How could we make sure the government represents its citizens? That's exactly what a bunch of guys did when they founded the United States. In 1987 *Time* magazine honored the two hundredth birthday of the U.S. Constitution with this description of the country's beginnings:

As Lincoln said at Gettysburg, the U.S. was a new nation, "brought forth" and dedicated to a proposition, an idea. America was not a pre-existing cohesion, like Japan, which had its origins back in the Shinto mists of its prehistory. America was a conscious creation of the mind, of science. It was creatively assembled out of ideas, traditions and genes rounded up elsewhere and unloaded in a New World.[1]

The men who dreamed up this country were not satisfied with **what is.** They dared to ask *what if?* Their answers to that question changed the world.

I Have a Dream

On August 28, 1963, thousands of people gathered in front of the Lincoln Memorial in Washington, D.C., to hear speeches from several civil rights leaders. The keynote speaker, a preacher from Atlanta, Georgia, shared his dream of racial equality. Here's a portion of the speech "I Have a Dream" by Martin Luther King, Jr. Notice how he compares **what is** to *what if?*, leading us along in his dream from reality to possibility:

I have a dream that one day on the red hills of Georgia, sons of former slaves and sons of

1. Lance Morrow, "The Ark of America," *Time*, July 6, 1987, p. 27.

former slave-owners will be able to *sit down together at the table of brotherhood.*

I have a dream that one day, even the state of Mississippi, a state sweltering with the heat of injustice, sweltering with the heat of oppression, will be transformed into *an oasis of freedom and justice.*

I have a dream my four little children will one day live in a nation where they will not be judged by the color of their skin but *by content of their character.* I have a dream today!

I have a dream that one day, down in Alabama, with its vicious racists, with its governor having his lips dripping with the words of interposition and nullification, that one day, right there in Alabama, *little black boys and black girls will be able to join hands with little white boys and white girls as sisters and brothers.* I have a dream today!

I have a dream that one day every valley shall be *exalted,* every hill and mountain shall be *made low,* the rough places shall be *made plain,* and the crooked places shall be *made straight and the glory of the Lord will be revealed and all flesh shall see it together.*

Less than five years later, King died from an assassin's bullet. But the dream outlived the dreamer (good dreams always do). As his widow, Coretta Scott King, put it: "The forces of repression and brutality can slay the dreamer, but not the dream."

The people who change the world are the ones who dream—who dare to raise themselves above **what is** and ask *what if?*

- *What if* you could prevent a child in the Third World from dying of hunger?
- *What if* schools were filled with teachers who had a passion to see students learn to think and question and strive to change the world?
- *What if* you discovered a cure for muscular dystrophy?
- *What if* you figured out a way to save the lives of East African children by purifying their bacteria-laden water source?

This world is filled with horrible stuff: hatred, disease, greed, hunger, and loneliness. We desperately need people who are willing to ask *what if?* Here are some steps to help you dream.

Take Time to Dream

As little kids, we dreamed and imagined constantly. But somewhere along the way to adulthood, worries about **what is** crowd out our thoughts of *what if?* For example, my third-grade teacher asked me what I wanted to be when I grew up. I said I wanted to be a jet test pilot. A week later the school nurse called me into her office to inform me that I could never be a jet test pilot because I was color-blind. **What is** came crashing in.

Has **what is** crowded out your dreams? Push back. Give your imagination room to exercise daily. Push aside your tower of textbooks every so often to read a fairy tale, fantasy, or science fiction story. Push the TV's off button, and write in a journal instead. If you discipline yourself to dream regularly, dreams of a better world will come.

Start a Dream Team

The safest way to keep your dreams alive is to tell them to others. Find other dreamers and dream with them regularly. A team of trustworthy friends can help you fulfill your dreams.

I have my own dream team—good friends who listen to my ideas. I respect them and know that if they believe a dream is wrong or misguided, they'll tell me. If it's a good dream, they encourage me and even join in the pursuit.

How Well Do You Dream?

Take a minute to ponder these *what if*'s:

What if the world stopped spinning? Would we fall off? Would there be night and day? Seasons? Storms?

What if humans had three fingers on each hand? Would we have a number system based on six? If so, we'd have no 800 numbers and no "high fives." Name three other things we wouldn't have.

What if all personal computers could speak and understand spoken words fluently? Would they still have keyboards? Would they talk to each other when no one else was in the room? What kind of accent would they have? A male or female voice? Could they sense anger or joy in your voice? If such a computer were printing your spoken words, how would it know when to type exclamation and question marks?

What if dogs could talk? Would they create their own society? Would they start their own TV stations? What would the remote control look like? What would be their favorite shows?

Dream Good

At Disneyland there's a ride that lets you power a small boat around a waterway. When I was a little kid, the ride was a thrill because I thought I was actually maneuvering the vessel through the killer rapids. Later on, at that special age when ramming the boat into the rocks becomes one's *goal*, I discovered that the steering was controlled by an underwater track—I was safe no matter what I did with the wheel.

But dreams aren't like a Disneyland ride. There are no hidden tracks to keep them magically on course. Seemingly good dreams can turn into nightmares. It's up to you to steer your dreams right.

In Greek mythology, a guy named Midas wished for the golden touch—the ability to turn ordinary objects to gold just by touching them. The dream turned to a nightmare when his touch turned the people he loved into statues of soulless metal. As you pursue your dreams, remember that they just may come true. So consider carefully

10

what impact they'll have on you and others. Are the dreams good? Will they make the world a better place?

Dream Again

It's not enough to come up with a dream and then pursue it. You've got to keep dreaming—shaping existing dreams and developing new ones. I'd love to say that this book is a dream I've had for years. Actually, much of this book started out as some speeches I gave a few years ago. I put together a book proposal entitled *Secrets of Success*. The publisher rejected it.

I reworked the direction of the book, added some chapters, and called it *Walking Upside Down*. But something still wasn't right, so I kept working on it. I discovered that each of the chapters was really about my favorite subject: making a difference. So I refocused the chapters, added the Appendix, and changed the title to *How to Rearrange the World*.

But wait—there's more. I wrote proposals for three other books the same year: all were rejected. But I haven't given up on them, either. I just know that many of my dreams aren't all that great, so I've got to keep dreaming (and dreaming and dreaming) to find the ones that will work best.

If you have dreams, keep replaying them in your mind. Edit and add to them constantly. Then dream new and different dreams, knowing that many of them *won't* come true. But if you keep at it, the best ones will.

Now that you're excited about dreaming, let me depress you for a moment. Even if you do all of this—take time to dream, start a dream team, dream good, and dream again—it won't make an ounce of difference in this world. Dreams are like blueprints: they're pictures of the building and not the building itself. If you want to see the real thing, you're going to have to construct it. The rest of the chapters can show you how to transform your dreams into reality.

Practice Dreaming

Here are some exercises to help you develop your dreamability. Depending on how much dreaming you want to do, you can spend from twenty minutes to a few hours on one of them. You can even get a friend to join you.

Dream House

Design your dream house—money is no object. Where is it located? What does it look like? Does it have an indoor pool? Are there water slides from every bedroom? How about a rope swing from your room to the kitchen in case you get hungry in the middle of the night? Does the garage convert to a drive-in theater? You get the idea. Lay it out on paper. Draw the floor plan on graph paper; sketch the interior and exterior views.

New School

You've been in school long enough to have your own ideas about education. So, what if the school board asked you to design a *new* school? They've given you permission to design the buildings and classrooms, hire the teachers, decide on the subjects that will be taught, and come up with the daily schedule. Prepare a presentation for them. Make posters showing the school's layout, including a sketch of the typical classroom. Write a short description of the new school, explaining what's wrong with most schools and how this school solves those problems. Come up with a list of qualifications for hiring teachers, a class schedule, and a list of courses you'll offer.

(Your Name) land

Walt Disney dreamed up Disneyland. Now it's your turn. Where is your amusement park? How big is it? Does it have a theme (water park, movie studio, marine life, Antarctic expedition, Albanian village)? What does it look like? What are the major attractions in it? Design a couple of the rides. Draw out the whole park.

Rose, Bud

While at a fancy dessert party, you bump into a buffet table. Oh, no—a rose blossom from a floral decoration falls into a chocolate fondue pot. When you fish the flower from the sauce, the idea for a new smash hit candy sensation hits you: chocolate-covered rosebuds! It's time to dream. Are rosebuds *edible*? What about pesticides or other chemicals? Do different colors and varieties taste differently? How do you package them? What do you call this new product? Do you sell it through candy stores or floral shops? After the initial success of the rosebuds, what related products could you follow up with?

Now sketch a package idea for selling your product. Make a list of possible slogans for it. Lay out a magazine ad. Write a script for a TV commercial.

DREAM WEEK

Take five minutes every day this week to exercise your dreaming.

MONDAY   Make a short list of some of the answers you've had to the question, What do you want to be when you grow up? What made you choose some of those things? What made you change your mind? Now what do you want to be? Why? What are you doing to pursue it?

TUESDAY   Write out your biggest dream (other than career). How long have you had the dream? On a scale of zero to 100 percent, what do you think is the likelihood of your dream coming true? What can you do *today* to take a step closer to it? Do it!

WEDNESDAY Make a list of your other dreams. Write "Dreams" at the top of the page and date it. At the bottom of the page, add the instruction "Write a new list now." Then hide the list where you're likely to stumble across it again in a year or so (maybe your clean sock drawer). The next time you find it, read it and check off any dreams that have come true. Then write a new list, date it, and hide it with the old one. Keep doing this every year—it will become a wonderful record of your dreams through the years.

THURSDAY   Share one of your dreams with a trusted friend.

FRIDAY   Ask a friend to share a dream with you. Treat it with care.

SATURDAY   Ask a parent if any of his or her dreams have come true. What was it? How long did it take?

SUNDAY   The ancient Jewish king, David, said this: "Delight yourself . . . in the LORD, and He shall give you the desires of your heart." Does this mean God will give you anything—money, power, fame—if you do what David said? How do you delight yourself in the Lord? (Psalm 37:4)

2

Be a Child

It's starting to look like Munchkin Land. Fifth graders wearing makeup, perfume, and high heels. Third graders sporting $90 shoes. Second graders cussing like pirates. Two-year-olds learning to spell. And my one-year-old nephew has a pair of Nikes. Why is everyone in such a hurry to spell, swear, and smell like adults?

The pressure to grow up is greater than ever. The years in high school used to be a time when you could prepare yourself for adulthood. Not anymore. By the time you graduate, many of your peers will have taken up smoking, drinking, using cocaine, and having sexual intercourse. You're the same group of kids who were playing with troll dolls and Tonka trucks eight years earlier.

Many of the thrills and vices of adulthood are now available to you; no need to wait in line for the magic age of eighteen or twenty-one. Likewise, the things that *used to be* teenage privileges are now accessible to children. Look at money. Years ago, children didn't care about it; teenagers needed it; adults had it. Now, children are bombarded by TV ads convincing them that they need the toys only money can buy, your friends earn heaps of it through part-time jobs and hefty allowances, and most adults are in debt.

Exposure to violence comes earlier, too. Once upon a time adults protected children from seeing it. Teenagers were permitted to see horror films. And the only ones who *committed* violence were adults. Nowadays, children are exposed to it, teenagers commit it, and adults get rich producing films and TV programs about it.

The biggest downshift in privileges and vices has happened in the area of sex. Thirty years ago, children found it disgusting, teenagers got to learn about it, and adults did it. Today, children get to learn about it through TV, movies, music, and school; teenagers are doing it; and many adults are disgusted with it!

More than Pampers

What effect is this downshift in thrills and vices having on *you?* The problem with all this early exposure to "adult" stuff is not what it does to you but what it *takes away.*

Growing up too fast can steal from you priceless pieces of childhood that you were meant to keep all your life. I'm not talking about Pampers and Barbie dolls, thumb sucking, and drawing on the walls with crayons (although sometimes I really miss my built-in crayon sharpener). It's deeper than that.

Being a child has more to do with the inside than the outside. Children are simple, innocent, modest, forgiving, friendly, unprejudiced. You had each of these valuable traits as a kid. Do you still have them?

World Changers Are Children at Heart

If you study people who have made a big difference in the world, you discover that childlike qualities are among their greatest strengths. They've somehow managed to hold onto their youthful idealism while others have traded theirs for skepticism, hopelessness, and a preoccupation with **what is.**

You're at an age when these priceless qualities are in grave danger. If you intend to make a difference in this world, you need to guard these pieces of childhood with your life.

Modest and Messy

The good old days. The days when you didn't even *think* about your looks. You could wake up precisely five minutes before it was time to leave for school. That didn't leave much room to get ready, but there really wasn't much to do. Pick out clothes to wear? No need—the ones you wore yesterday are conveniently laid out for you on the floor.

Take a shower? No, you just had one three days ago, and besides, there's a water shortage. Brush your teeth? You did that last month.

Comb your hair? Why bother? It stays in place by itself from all the grease that has accumulated since the last time you washed it (in June, when you had to dress up and go see your cousin Calvin from Covina get married).

Those days are gone. You're acutely aware of yourself and concerned about how others see you. Now if you showed up at school dressed and groomed as just described, you might be quarantined as a public health hazard. There's nothing wrong with this self-awareness—looking good makes you feel confident, which helps you treat others better. But when concern for your physical and social appearance becomes your top priority, you get into trouble.

Here's how. People who stare at themselves long enough begin to see a distorted picture. They look in the mirror and see fat where there is none, so they starve themselves. They look into a beautiful face and see ugly, so they mask it with thick coats of makeup. Worst of all, they're too busy looking at themselves to take much notice of anyone else. This preoccupation with the *outside* leaves them feeling empty and worthless on the inside. Which may be why it's called *vanity*, a term that comes from the Latin word for "empty."

Vanity: Symptoms and Cures

Vanity is very contagious. If you spend most of your time among people who make appearance their priority, you'll probably catch the same illness. Once you have it, you develop an incredible dependency on mirrors. You become addicted to compliments—you never seem to get enough.

Like a drug, you develop a tolerance for compliments that used to make you feel good. They just aren't potent anymore. You become filled with self-doubt to the point that you don't believe people when they say nice things to you. Someone tells you that you look great, and you think, *She's just saying that to make me feel better.*

Vanity is an adult trait. Little kids don't care about appearances. They laugh, cry, scream, explore nostrils, scratch behinds, and run around naked in public. They're modest—not in the reserved sense but in the unpretentious sense. They're so busy living, they don't have time to stare in the mirror.

It's not easy to hold onto childlike modesty in a culture so caught up in appearances, yet it is possible. First, there are a few things you *don't* have to do.

- Throw a tantrum in the supermarket cereal aisle.
- Streak naked through the mall.
- Go a month without bathing.
- Pick your nose during an oral report.

But there are a couple of things you *can* do to hold on to modesty.

Step off the vain train. If you spend most of your time with a group of people who make appearance their priority, you're bound for the same destination. It's an expensive ticket: you have to keep buying the right shoes and clothes and jewelry and albums and toys to stay aboard.

Stop and consider. Do you really want to stay on this train? If the cost—in money, time, and self-image—is too great, step off NOW.

Find inside friends. An inside friend isn't caught up in your appearance. He cares more about what you're like on the inside. This is not to say that he ignores your appearance. He knows this is important, too, so he compliments you honestly—yet he isn't afraid to slip you a breath mint or point out the mustard on your face. He cares about you enough to help you look your best. He's not going to let you look funny unless, of course, that's what you really want to do.

But the primary target of his compliments is

your character. If you're a good listener, he tells you that. Often. If he's impressed with your honesty or sense of humor or ability to cheer people, he's not afraid to say it to your face. The crazy thing is, you have to believe him because he's taken the time to know you. He's not flattering you just to make you feel good—he's telling you the truth. And deep inside you know it.

The best way to find inside friends is to be one. Every day, make it a goal to encourage, praise, and affirm your friends. You'll discover that as they gain self-confidence, they'll spend less time in front of the mirror and more time encouraging you.

The End of Innocence

It's hard to believe, but you probably lived for years without ever thinking about sex. Up to this point, the majority of your life has been spent without concern or care for sexuality. When I first learned what sex involved, I thought, *Ugh! Why would* anyone *want to do* that*?!*

My, how time flies. Now it's hard to make it through a day and *not* think about sex. Try it. Don't watch TV—there are about twenty thousand implied sexual acts on television each year.[1] The average time from introduction to intercourse is measured in *minutes*.

Whatever you do, *don't* stand in the supermarket checkout line and read the magazine and tabloid covers: "Sex with a Younger Man," "Cheating on Your Lover," and "I Made Love to an Alien and Bore His Child."

The music store is definitely out of the question. Here's an informal inventory of band names in the spring of 1990: at least thirteen bands named after male genitals, four after sperm, eight after abortion, one after a vaginal infection, ten for various sex acts, and eight containing the *f* word.[2]

C. S. Lewis put it this way:

> Suppose you came to a country where you could fill a theatre by simply bringing a covered plate on to the stage and then slowly lifting the cover so as to let every one see, just before the

1. *Parade* magazine, December 18, 1988.
2. John Leo, "Rock 'n' Roll's Hatemongering," *U.S. News & World Report*, March 19, 1990, p. 17.

lights went out, that it contained a mutton chop or a bit of bacon, would you not think that in that country something had gone wrong with the appetite for food?[3]

Beyond Sex

Sex can be wonderful. But it doesn't deserve the attention we give it in our culture and media. Contrary to the popular images, sex is more than bodies slamming together.

When you have sex with someone, you give away a part of your *self*. It's a beautiful gift to someone who'll cherish it. But if the relationship ends, that part of you is thrown away. With most people, the pain is intense. Those who've given themselves away a lot tend to grow numb to the hurt. If you haven't personally experienced this, you can

3. *Mere Christianity* (New York: Macmillan, 1960), p. 89.

probably look around your school to find people who have. (Show me a person who sleeps around, and I'll show you someone with low self-esteem.)

It's kind of like gambling. When you first sit down at the table, you have lots of chips, and you can afford to make some foolish bets. But it doesn't take long before your chips are down, and every loss cuts deeper into your pile. The pressure of losing it all changes your ability to make choices. You either "go for broke"—risking it all on stupid bets—or freeze up and refuse to play at all.

Some people have given themselves in so many relationships that they have almost nothing left to give. Now they're desperate, and they continue to make foolish choices with relationships.

I know this is an awfully dim picture of sex, but you've already seen several thousand pictures that completely ignore the innocence and self-image issues, so I thought I'd give you an opposing viewpoint. If you want to hold on to your childhood innocence in this area, try the following tips.

Change, turn, close. Let's say you're on a diet, so you've decided to cut out sweets for a while. But half the songs on your favorite radio station are about chocolate. Three TV shows in one night feature thin characters devouring bowls of ice cream. And you're reading a novel about a woman who can't stop eating Reese's peanut butter cups. Sure, you can be exposed to all these sweets and still have the self-control to stay on your diet. But it makes life a bit more difficult. It's perfectly reasonable to change the radio station, turn off the TV, and close the book.

The same is true for sex. If you want to limit the dozens of times you're exposed to the topic daily, there's no law against changing the radio station, turning off the TV, or closing a book and reading a different one. I say this because, amazing as it sounds, some people don't understand that this is an intelligent response. Maybe they've spent so much time fighting for the freedom to read, listen to, and watch what they please that the idea of imposing their own limits seems ridiculous. It's the difference between what you have the right to do and what you have the responsibility to do.

Procrastinate. Why hurry to do today what you can take your time to enjoy for nearly the rest of your life? Sex isn't a course you need for graduation. You don't lose your eligibility if you postpone it. In fact, the earlier you start, the more likely you are to have serious relationship problems later on.

If you decide to postpone sex, you won't be alone. You hear lots of news reports about the high percentage of teens having sex, which are backed up by the stories you hear in the locker room. What you don't hear about is the large but silent percentage of teenagers who don't even date or fall in love until after they graduate from high school. Most are normal, healthy, good-looking people who either aren't interested in dating yet or haven't met anyone they care to get involved with. They're not as conspicuous as their dating peers because they don't announce their condition (HEY, EVERYONE, I'VE NEVER BEEN KISSED). They prefer to just relax, let nature take its course, and concentrate on the things that are important to them. Join the club.

Talk and draw. If you're in a dating relationship now, talk to your partner. Hear each other's expectations, and draw clear, realistic limits. Respect his or her limits, and demand that he or she respect yours.

What to Keep, What to Discard

You may look at these traits and realize that you've already lost them. But it's not too late to get them back. That is one of the great things about being your age: you don't have to reach back very far to find them again. To adults, being like a child is tough. We've blocked out much of our childhood, and we find it difficult to remember how we felt. You are so much closer to it.

As you run pell-mell at adulthood, shedding childhood as fast as you can, hurrying to look, act, smell, and talk like someone more grown-up than yourself, just . . . STOP: take a breath, and decide which parts of yourself to keep and which to throw away. What childlike quality are you about to toss away that you'll need to change the world?

Practice Childlikeness

Here are some activities and exercises to help you hold on to your childlike qualities throughout life.

Child Labor
The best way to regain your childlikeness is to hang around those who still have it. Get a job at a day-care center; be a day camp counselor during the summer; volunteer as a children's coach. Find out what makes them tick: their dreams, heroes, goals, perceptions of the world, likes and dislikes.

Kids' Books
Some of the best literature in the world is written for children. Reading stories that you first

heard as a kid can help you remember your childhood. You'll rediscover that children's literature is written to appeal to a child's clear and simple sense of right and wrong. The stories are filled with issues of justice, mercy, love, sacrifice, courage, and integrity. In a confusing world of grays, a kid's book can help reclarify what's important.

Eyewitness

Interview your parents about what you were like as a young child. Ask them to describe when they discovered certain personality traits and the significant experiences that helped shape who you are. Get out picture albums and scrapbooks. Look for old schoolwork, report cards, and souvenirs. Take a walk through your elementary school. Try to remember what was important to you, your heroes, goals, and dreams.

Let Go

Let go of an "adult" behavior or habit you've developed. Stop drinking, smoking, or having sex. The problem isn't that these things might make you more "grown up"—they don't. It's that they steal your *youth*.

KID WEEK

MONDAY   Ask a parent to describe how you were as a child and how you've changed—good *and* bad.

TUESDAY   Ask a longtime friend to do the same thing. Ask, "What do you miss about the 'old' me? What do you see as an improvement?"

WEDNESDAY Inside day: make an effort to look on the inside of each person you speak to today. Affirm the individual's character in some way whenever possible. Oh, yeah, and no put-downs.

THURSDAY Conduct a sex count. Carry a piece of paper around today and mark each time you see or hear a sexual message: someone talking, writing, or singing about sex, or scenes of actual or implied sex in photos, in drawings, or on the screen. It's like listening for "um's"—you never realize how many there are until you start counting.

FRIDAY Write down your sexual standards. What are your limits of physical intimacy at various levels of a relationship: dating, steady, engagement? If you're dating someone now, talk about this together.

SATURDAY Take a few minutes to observe little kids at a playground or shopping mall.

SUNDAY Go on a media fast. No TV, videos, movies, radio, music, magazines, or books. Think, draw, play, build, talk, listen, or nap.

3
Stand

I was seventeen and working a temporary job during the last two weeks of my summer. The boss, a friendly man in his mid-thirties, decided one night to treat the staff to a pizza dinner, so about twenty of us squeezed into a few cars and drove to the restaurant. When we walked out to the parking lot after dinner, it appeared to me that the boss had had too much beer to drive safely. I considered keeping silent about it—why cause a fuss?—but then I saw all those people getting into his car. So I opened my big mouth.

He was not pleased. He was sober, he said, and there was no reason why he couldn't drive his own car. I tried to persuade him to let someone else drive, but he brushed me aside and got behind the wheel. That's when I took the keys.

What happened next is all fuzzy to me now, but I do remember him telling me, in essence, that I was a punk kid who didn't have the right to work for him and then start telling him what to do. He pointed out that I was making a fool of myself in front of all those people. Then he snatched his keys from my hand, started the car, and drove off.

Embarrassed and humiliated, I climbed into another car. On the ride back, I thought, *Why didn't anyone else come to my side? Was I the only one with the guts to say something? Or was I just stupid for trying? Was I wrong?* I learned one lesson: taking a stand can be a lonely job.

Let's face it. Most of us are comfortable leaving things just the way they are. We're conformists. If they handed out report cards for living, most people would get straight *C*'s:

Compliant
Comfortable
Conforming
Complacent
Cattle
Calm
Cozy
Coma

There's nothing wrong with conformity. Unless . . . the crowd you're conforming to is headed the wrong way. Then it's time to stand up and say, "Hey! Something is wrong!"

World Changers Take a Stand

Back to that report card thing. Although most people seem satisfied with a *C* average in life, world changers shoot for straight *A*'s:

Ask
Alert
Alarm
Assert
Agitate
Advocate
Alone
Alive

Of all these *A*'s, the most important is *ask*.

World changers make a career out of asking, "What's wrong with this picture?" If you look around, you'll see lots of pictures that just don't look right. Something is out of proportion or simply doesn't belong. Here are a few examples.

Date Rape

Here's a messed-up picture. Some guys go out on dates and then force the girls to have sex with them. Some figure that they've *earned* the sex: "What do you mean you won't go to bed with me? I bought you *dinner!*"

I just don't get it. If you think sex is purchased, you're confusing a prostitute with a date. All these guys who force their dates to have sex—where were they during manners week in nursery school?[1] Date rape is a horrible distortion of a beautiful picture.

Racism

Here's another picture I don't get. I thought about it today as I was running on the beach near my house. I passed a lot of dogs, including a pair of German shepherds, a family of huskies, and a gang of white Labradors. I tried to imagine what racism would look like to them.

They'd call it *breedism*. The German shepherds would growl breedist slurs at the huskies, like "Hey, *sled dogs*—mush home!" The huskies would take out their anger on the white Labs: "Look! Peroxide blondes!" They'd form violent breed packs; innocent poodles and pound dogs would be bloodied on street corners, victims of run-by bitings. Since they have no fingers, there would be no graffiti. Instead, they'd mark their turf in more natural ways. The horrors of breedism.

But the behavior of these dogs at the beach makes breedism hard to imagine. The main problem is that they don't seem to be aware of their

1. In case you were absent that week, here's a review:
   A. *No one* has the right to touch your body without your permission.
   B. That right *cannot* be purchased—not with money, not with attention.
   C. When someone tells you not to touch her and you do it anyway, it's *assault*.

41

differences. In fact, the opposite is true: the arrival of a dog of any brand is grounds for celebration—tails swinging, tongues slathering, a festival of yipping and skipping and sniffing and digging. Sure, there's an occasional exchange of growls, but these seem to be personality clashes rather than outbursts of breedism.

I know this is a ridiculous illustration. But so is racism.

AIDS

Some people claim that AIDS is God's specific punishment for homosexuals. If that were true, God would be sexist—lesbians are hardly affected.

God would also be getting the names mixed up because many gay men don't have AIDS, while children born to mothers with AIDS are being punished in their stead.

How can we begin to look for solutions when we're not even looking at a clear picture of the problem?

More Questions

There are hundreds of distorted pictures out there. Look around you and ask, "What's wrong with this picture?" You'll see the distortions if you do. But asking what's wrong is just the first step. To make a stand for something, you've got to ask a few other questions, too.

Am I qualified? To encourage people to vote in the 1990 elections, MTV recruited big-name musicians to perform in its "Rock the Vote" commercials. There was just one problem—some of the stars telling us to vote weren't even registered! They weren't qualified to tell others to stand because they hadn't taken their own advice. The big word here is *hypocrisy*.

Jesus put it this way: pull the log out of your own eye, then you'll be able to pull the splinter out of your neighbor's. If you want to be qualified to stand against a teacher's unfair grading policies, first give up your own cheating. To qualify for a

stand against hunger, first give some of your money to an organization that's doing something about the problem.

What's the price? The sad state of our world ensures that you'll have plenty of causes to stand for. In fact, you'll have too many. If you don't choose carefully, you'll spend all your time racing from one cause to another, trying to make a difference in all of them and making little difference in any of them.

You can't fix every picture. You can't fight for every just cause. Choose your battles with care—stick with causes your heart compels you to stand for. When other worthy causes come along, measure their cost in how they'll affect your primary mission. If you can't afford to fight for them, don't. Channel the frustration of not being able to fight for these causes into a fight you're already committed to.

What's my reason? Right now it's cool to have a cause. Most big-time musicians and actors support some cause or another, and they use their popularity to promote it. A few years ago the cool cause was world hunger. Unfortunately, the fad faded long before the hunger. The new cool cause became homeless people. Then AIDS. Then the environment—and a dozen other issues vying for popularity.

The problem with these cause fads is that lots of people join them not to support the cause but to *conform* to what's cool. Notice that we're back to the *C*'s on life's report card.

Some people stand up to sell concert tickets, compact discs, or colas. They stand up to cause chaos or to conform to the cool crowd or to call attention to themselves.

World changers stand up only when their hearts tell them that something is desperately wrong with the status quo—and that remaining seated and silent would be a sin. When you're considering standing for a cause, ask yourself, What's my reason? If your conscience has no good answer, stay seated. But if something inside you cries out to be heard, stand up.

I haven't told you the ending to that story about my boss and the car keys. I left for college the next day without having to face him again. But over the holidays we happened to cross paths. Actually, I had spotted him and hoped he hadn't seen me.

No such luck. He marches up (I'm thinking, *Here we go again*), shakes my hand, and says, basically, that I had guts to do what I did and that he likes guts and would I like to work for him full-time next summer?

I worked for him that summer and the next one, too.

STAND WEEK

MONDAY Read the Declaration of Independence. No kidding—it's one of the all-time greatest stands.

TUESDAY Look around you for someone who has taken a stand. Tell him you appreciate what he did.

WEDNESDAY Now look for someone who's being treated unfairly—being falsely blamed, not given a fair turn, or the target of prejudice. Stick up for her.

Dear Mr. President,

I'm writing you because I believe it's important that you know what young people like me are thinking these days.

THURSDAY   Write a note to the president. Let him know how you feel about an issue you believe needs his attention. Here's his address: The White House, 1600 Pennsylvania Avenue NW, Washington, DC 20500.

FRIDAY   Ask a friend to describe a time he stood up for something he believed in.

SATURDAY   Ask a parent the same question.

SUNDAY   Read about one of the all-time great stands in history, found in the Bible—the third chapter in the book of Daniel.

4
Question Authority

This chapter is a scary one to write. I can't help thinking that any minute now, the Word Police are going to show up. They'll break down my door and put a gun to my head and a finger to my keyboard. Then they'll watch as the delete key swallows, one letter at a time, this whole chapter.

Later on people will ask me, "The book has a chapter 3 and a chapter 5—what happened to *4?*" And I'll say, "Don't ask questions. Sit down, shut up, and do as you're told." Which is exactly what the Word Police will tell me to say when they're finished with me and my chapter.

But then I remember an important fact: there are no Word Police. I'm free to tell you to question authority because others before me had the guts to question authority—and fought for the freedom to do it. Watch this. *Question authority.* (Door still on hinges.) *Question authority.* (No gun.) *Question authority.* (Ha! I'm still here.)

But just because you have the *freedom* to question authority, don't assume that there aren't dire consequences for exercising that freedom. Questioning authority is serious business, and you better be willing to pay the price. I remember many times as a kid when I questioned authority and got in a heap of trouble for it.

Like in third grade, when I was sent to the principal's office for stabbing Sara Jane Clairmont in the hand with a pencil (hey, she started it). When Mr. Harris told me to apologize to her, I said I didn't have to unless she was made to apologize to me. That's when he called my mom. I think I've repressed what happened after that.

Or when I got put on restriction for a week (for setting the house on fire, as I recall), questioned the fairness of such a harsh sentence, and got a second week for my efforts.

The temptation to question authority is great when you're a teenager because you're *surrounded* by authority figures: parents, teachers, coaches, school officials, police, bosses—and just about any other adult who feels like telling you what to do. And let's face it: some adults are experts at making ridiculous, pointless, arbitrary, unfair, or impossible rules that seem custom-made for defying.

Some teenagers have an attitude about *all* authority, good and bad. Like a rock climber scaling a cliff, they question authority "because it's there." They don't have a problem with a particular rule or issue—they have a problem with respect for others. Instead of learning to *question* authority, they choose to . . .

ignore authority

or *fight* authority

or *despise* authority.

At the other end of the spectrum are students who always do as they're told—even when what they're told is wrong. They're like robots. You can tell them what to do, and they'll do it without a thought. You can tell them what to believe, and they'll believe it without question. So rather than *question* authority, they . . .

worship authority

or *live in fear* of authority.

Both of these extremes—rebellion and blind compliance—are dangerous. There *is* a proper place for questioning authority. And if you want to make a difference in this world, you've got to find that place.

World Changers Question Authority

If you look carefully at people who've made a big difference in this world, you'll see that they've learned to question authority wisely. Here are some steps you can take to question wisely.

Show Respect

One way to show respect is to do what someone tells you. That's why, when you decide to question authority, you've got to do it with respect.

Let's say you work at a store. When someone calls to speak to your boss and he doesn't want to take the call, he asks you to tell the person he's not there. In short, he's asking you to lie for him. You have at least three choices:

1. Do as you're told.
2. Tell him he doesn't have the right to make you lie for him.
3. Tell him that you wouldn't feel right about saying that, and suggest an alternative such as, "He's not available."

53

If you choose the first option, well . . . what can I say? Maybe read chapter 3 again.

If you choose the second option, you're doing the right thing—but you're doing it backward. You're questioning his right to tell you what to do—a right you *gave* him when you accepted the job.

The third option goes straight to the real issue, which is your personal duty to do what's right. If he's a decent boss, he'll respect your view—even if he doesn't share it. Show respect and you'll get respect.

Obey the Higher Authority

Questioning authority is not a matter of disobedience. It's a matter of obeying a higher authority over a lower authority.

Let's say that in the previous example, your boss insists that you do as he tells you. You believe that doing so would be a lie. You also believe that God has told you not to lie.

The wise choice is to obey the higher authority—in this case, God. So you say something like, "You're telling me to do something that God has told me not to do. I choose to obey Him."

When I read this last paragraph, it sounds strange to me. That's because hardly anyone ever says such things. It's a rare person who *admits* that she's willfully obeying someone higher than herself. Disobedience is cool. Obedience looks silly. But world changing is not about *looking* good; it's about *doing* what's right.

When you're tempted to question authority, figure out whose authority you're going to obey.

Question Yourself

One of the biggest problems with obeying a higher authority is that you can remember many times when you chose to disobey a higher authority just because it was more convenient—calling in "sick," fudging your hours, giving freebies to friends.

That is why changing the world starts in your heart. What right do you have to question the authority of others when you don't question your own authority? Do what's right in your own life, then work for what's right in the lives of others.

QUESTION WEEK

MONDAY   Make a table of authorities: whose authority will you obey over all others? Who's next? Where do parents, teachers, friends, siblings, God, and the government fit in?

TUESDAY   Say you're sorry. Think back and find an instance where you failed to show respect for a parent, teacher, or other adult with authority. Apologize to that person today.

WEDNESDAY   Using your table of authorities as a guide, find an area in your life where you frequently disregard your own table. Why?

THURSDAY   What's one thing you can do this week to correct this inconsistency?

FRIDAY   Pick an area where your behavior isn't consistent with your table of authorities. What will you do this week to correct that?

SATURDAY   You're an authority figure for
            others. Who? Make a list of people
            who see you as an authority figure
            (friends, siblings, coworkers). What
            one thing can you do this week to
            be an authority worthy of respect?
            Be specific.

SUNDAY   Find and read this verse in the
            Bible: 1 Timothy 2:1–2. Take two
            minutes right now to do what it
            says.

5

Think Again

I remember a single question that haunted me throughout school: Why do I need to learn *this*? A few times I asked teachers, "Can you give me one good reason why this is important to know?" I never got a good answer.

In eighth grade their answer was, "You need to know this for high school." When I asked my high-school teachers, they told me the stuff I was learning was necessary to get into college. In college I stopped asking the question—I was too busy studying to pass the exams to get the credits to graduate. Now it's been ten years since I graduated from college, and I finally found the answer.

The reason I studied Spanish in high school was that one day I'd have the opportunity to help build an orphanage in Mexico. I'd need to know the language to be able to communicate. And if I had *any* clue of how frustrating it is to be unable to understand the stories and jokes and questions of a Spanish-speaking child, I would have studied Spanish with a passion.

I didn't know why I took geometry and algebra and physics until we had to design the sewage system and roof for the orphanage. The Pythagorean theorem was no longer a test question; it was a calculation used to keep kids safe in a storm.

I didn't know it then, but I studied English so I could write money-raising proposals for worthy causes and articles and books to motivate people to make a difference. I thought it was for the *grade*.

I didn't understand that term papers and group projects and oral reports and heavy reading and study assignments were all there to prepare me for opportunities in which I could help change the world—*if* I had the organizational, interpersonal, intellectual, and communication skills to pull it off. And I was worried about my GPA. Silly me.

I didn't realize that someday I'd have things

burning inside me that I'd want to tell people (and the audacity to think that others would want to hear them); and if I didn't have the ability to think or write or speak or draw or organize, no one would ever hear me. *That's* why I went to school.

World Changers Think Hard and Often

I'd be a liar if I told you that I remember most of the things I learned in school. I'd fail a pop quiz at this moment if it had questions about gerunds, electrons, cosines, or the Marshall Plan. The long-term value of my education has been not *what I learned* but the *process of learning*. Somehow, in the process of listening, reading, discussing, writing, and cramming, I learned how to think.

Warning: although being a good *thinker* may help you get better grades, the two aren't always connected. In fact, it's possible to get wonderful grades without doing much thinking at all. In the worst case, high grades *may* reveal an average thinker who just happens to be . . .

- an aural learner (good at listening and remembering lectures).
- an excellent guesser on multiple-choice tests.
- good at cramming and memorizing.
- agreeable; doesn't question teacher or disrupt the lesson plan.
- skilled at cheating.

There's nothing wrong with good grades—they'll help you get into courses and schools where you can learn important things. But your good grades won't change the world; your good thinking will. Here are some tips to help you become a better thinker.

Play Offense

When it comes to learning, most people are like barnacles: they sit there and wait for the nutrition to wash into them. Forget this method! If you want to grow in your knowledge and abilities, go after your education with passion. Ask questions, read the book, and try to figure out what good this knowledge will be later on.

Mix Up Your Subjects

Schools divide learning into individual subjects, which you study for about fifty minutes at a time. But except for people who teach those subjects, nobody in the real world actually *applies* the subjects individually. Virtually any job, any project, or any career requires hundreds of skills in a dozen subjects.

Do the same thing in your studies. If you're putting together a geography report, design a chart to convey some of the numbers graphically. For a writing assignment, develop a mystery that can be solved using knowledge picked up from biology class.

For history class, choose the one hundred most important dates in American history, and group them as "good" or "bad." Then calculate the percentage of great moments occurring on a Tuesday; graph the correlation of tragedies and full moons; determine the probability of a future constitutional amendment occurring on the opening day of duck season. Okay, maybe not.

Bounce Things Around

Most people learn by playing catch. The teacher throws the knowledge at them, and they throw it back on the test. Boring. The best learning looks more like racquetball doubles. The teacher serves a question, you hit it back with an answer, then everyone starts taking swings in the discussion. Knowledge is bouncing off the walls, flying around the court. At the end of the game you're exhilarated and sweating.

If you want to become a better thinker, don't play catch with knowledge. When you read or hear something, write about it, talk about it, ask questions, and debate ideas with others. Bounce it around.

Apply It

The best way to retain knowledge is to use it as soon as you can. Use math skills to create a personal budget, make and track some investments, or manage your mom's checking account; at work, track sales figures, do bookkeeping, or calculate how many hours you'll have to work at minimum wage to become a billionaire. Use English and writing skills to keep a journal, write a family Christmas letter, or do a resume; at work, write advertising copy, put together a company newsletter, or write a plan to increase sales by giving away a Ferrari to every two thousandth customer who says something nice.

Think After School

Some of the most valuable knowledge isn't available in school. A good job, a volunteer position, or duties in a club or youth group teach you things you can't learn in a classroom. Learning outside school is generally more interesting, too: there's more racquetball-type learning and less catch because you're usually thinking and working with other people. (Before you get any silly ideas about quitting school, let me say that you need *both* kinds of education. If you quit one or ignore the other, you'll spend the rest of your life catching up.)

You're surrounded by teachers being paid to help you. Some are mediocre; a few are really bad. But most of your teachers know their subjects and their students, and they know how to teach. They long for students who are hungry to learn. They want to work with students who show a passion for learning because it reminds them of the passion they have for teaching—or once had. They're tired of playing catch—they're ready for some racquetball.

While you're still in school, make the most of it. Learn how to think. Then one day, maybe even today, when you have things burning inside that must be said, people will be able to hear you.

Practice Thinking

Learn to Write

Writing is not about essays and reports, grades and grammar. Writing is power. Virtually every influential message, event, or movement in this world begins with it. Films, speeches, articles, songs, letters, business proposals, news broadcasts, music videos, commercials, slogans, laws, amendments, contracts, stories, poems, philosophies—they all started as words. Until you learn to write well, you'll be very limited in your ability to make a difference in this world.

Unfortunately, there's a good chance that you'll

make it all the way through high school and college and *still* be a lousy writer. (I did, and now I'm trying to unlearn twenty years of bad habits.) Here are some tips to help you write well.

1. *Read good writing.* If you want to be good, study the best. Read as many classics as you can get your hands on.
2. *Don't write like a textbook.* Most teachers and textbook writers belong to the *academic* world, which has its own language and writing customs. Academics utilize multisyllabic words and/or expressions to facilitate a greater appearance of intellect. (Translation: they use big words to look smart.) Forget the flash. Just write so people can understand.
3. *Write in clear, short sentences.*[1]
4. *Learn grammar.* It's true that most people won't notice the difference. But a few people *will* notice—and they're the ones who have the power to hire, fire, publish, and produce. Learn their language.
5. *Write every day.* Keep a journal and write your thoughts each day, even if it's only a paragraph. If you get famous later on, you can use these notes for your autobiography.

---

1. Or as it says in the textbook, "When you write, do so in such a way that as few words as necessary are used to convey a clear meaning to the reader."

Cross-Train

At the beginning of the semester, find out what major papers or projects will be due for each class. Come up with a project that fits the needs of two or three of your classes. Then present the idea to those teachers and ask if they'll count the project in each class. Here's one example:

Full Access Water Park Proposal

Water parks are popping up all over the country. They have water slides, inner tube runs, and wave pools. But they're not well designed for people in wheelchairs. Put together a proposal to build a water park in your area that provides special services for people in wheelchairs.

The proposal is really a business plan, which you would submit to bankers, prospective business partners, the city, and others. Depending on the courses you were trying to get credit for, it might include the following:

- a description of the park and its unique accessibility (English)
- a short history of theme parks in the U.S. (history)
- site plans and renderings (drafting, art)
- a three-year budget and cash flow projection (math, business)

- an oral presentation to potential investors (speech)
- slide design, water flow, use of solar heating (physics)

THINK WEEK

MONDAY   Write one or two paragraphs about what you're thinking today. (Do this each day this week.)

TUESDAY   Ask at least one good question in each class today.

WEDNESDAY   Ask a respected teacher why she chose to teach; what's her favorite part of teaching; what's her worst.

DO YOU REALLY THINK THIS IS WHAT HE MEANT BY "READING A CLASSIC"?

THURSDAY   Pick up a classic book at the library. Read chapter 1. Finish the book in thirty days.

FRIDAY   Start a discussion with a friend about something you're learning in school.

SATURDAY   The government has passed a law: it can now force you to drop out of school and work as a manhole polisher—unless you can prove that every one of your classes is necessary to prepare you for the future. Write a paragraph for each of your classes, defending your need to take it.

SUNDAY   Go through a list of school assignments and find a couple that might be combined—a report that can be submitted for two different classes, a project that can be based on the knowledge you've acquired in another course.

6

Be Last

Lots of people measure life in letters and numbers:

It's SATs, MGM, & 4.0 GPA
   Making MVP, 3 TDs, or a 2.0 ERA
Wearing BKs, 501s, & 14k
   Pledging ΑΤΩ, ΚΚΓ, ΣΧ, ΑΓΔ
Driving XJS, 300Z, or CJ7 w/4WD
   Earning $200/hr & $1.5 mil (in CDs)
Scrambling, Fighting, Dying
   2B #1.

However we measure it, being first is the undeclared goal of most of our endeavors. We've been taught to reach for the top: in school and sports, in friendships and financial status, in possessions and power.

The hunger for supremacy is in our blood,

73

handed down to us through every generation clear back to our Uncle Ugh who fought to be King of the Primeval Hill. Between him and us lies an unbroken line of those who would be Emperor, Chief, Prime Minister, CEO, Class President, Big Cheese, Head Honcho, Top Dog, Prom Queen, or Grand Pooh-Bah.

Scrambling to be number one is an age-old pastime. It's also the antithesis of the most powerful world-changing strategy: being a servant. People who've made the biggest positive impact on the world have discarded this striving for supremacy. Instead, they've sought to be *last*.

It's really a backward idea. Logically, being number one and being able to make a difference in the world seem to go together:

- "If I were rich, I could use my money to do good things."

- "If I were famous, I could use my popularity to influence people."
- "If I were president, I could use my power to make changes."

And you're right—all these are true. But here's the problem. Striving to be number one is a full-time job. It takes up nearly all your time and attention, leaving you with little to give to others. And it's not like you ever really *arrive* at supremacy. No matter how rich or famous or successful you are, you can always be richer, more famous, or more successful. (Millionaires are just billionaire wannabe's.) Which translates into more time and attention devoted to yourself.

Staying on top is even harder than getting there. It's a grand game of King of the Hill—someone is always trying to topple you. Lots of times the people at the top become careless or corrupt and trip on their own power. Richard Nixon, Michael Milken, Donald Trump, Jim Bakker, Jimmy Swaggart, and Milli Vanilli all have one thing in common: their spectacular downfalls were caused by their own trip ups. They couldn't survive the altitude.

Good Service

I'm not saying that you shouldn't try to be your best at something. What counts is your motivation for getting there. Mother Teresa never set out to be world famous. She devoted herself to service and gained global respect for her sacrifices. The goal of Martin Luther King, Jr., was to help others—first in his own church, then in his town, then in his country. He was willing to sacrifice everything he had for the sake of others.

If you want to be number one at something, excel at serving others. Imagine that you were put on this planet to improve the lives of other people—to help them find more freedom, justice, happiness, health, and purpose. When you wake up in the morning, ask yourself, How can I make life better for the people I meet today? If that's your goal, you'll discover you have dozens of opportunities to achieve it.

I DIDN'T MEAN TO MAKE HER FAINT. ALL I DID WAS TELL HER I THOUGHT SHE WAS A GOOD TEACHER . . .

- Tell your parents you love them.
- Smile at a stranger.
- Tell a teacher you think she's doing a good job.
- Treat a cashier or clerk with respect. Say thank you.
- Let a friend know how much you appreciate his friendship.
- Write an encouraging note to someone who's going through a tough time.
- Help your sister do her chores.

- Instead of walking past a pile of litter, pick it up and throw it away.
- Send a postcard to a friend who's moved away.

The simplest gestures—smiles, hugs, hand-shakes, pats on the back—can help you fulfill your goal. Each says, "I'm happy you're alive." Simple comments—"Please," "Thank you," "Pardon me," "I'm sorry," "I like you," "I love you," "You're a good friend," "You yodel divinely," "How can I help?"—can change someone's day. Each expresses your willingness to put others first.

As you develop the attitude of a servant, you'll discover greater and more difficult opportunities to serve. But unless you learn to put yourself last in the small things, you'll never be able to make the big sacrifices later on.

When you can make these simple gestures of service without even thinking about it, start making greater sacrifices. In order to grow in your ability to change the world, you must constantly push yourself to serve people in ways that require sacrifice. As with physical exercise, it's "no pain, no gain."

SERVANT WEEK

MONDAY   Make 'em smile. Try to get a smile out of every person you meet today. (Hint: when you smile at people, they usually smile back.)

TUESDAY   Make your sister's bed. (Wait till she's out of it.)

WEDNESDAY Shine all your mother's shoes.

YES, SON, THEY'RE BEAUTIFULLY SHINY.
I CAN EVEN SEE MY REFLECTION...
WHICH IS REMARKABLE GIVEN THE FACT
THAT THEY ARE SUEDE SHOES.

THURSDAY Make and serve a formal dinner at your house. Dress as the servant. Serve the food, pour the drinks, and clean up the mess. (If you have a friend helping you, do the same thing at his house tomorrow night.)

FRIDAY Scour the kitchen. Clean behind the toaster and all those other places that don't get wiped often. Clean out the refrigerator—throw out all those scary containers of food that have been in there since last year.

SATURDAY Clean a friend's room.

SUNDAY Cook breakfast for your parents. Serve it to them in bed. (To make things easier, have them sleep in the kitchen.)

7

Mix It Up

You're a clone.

That's right: a clone. Let me prove it. You spend six hours a day, five days a week, with hundreds and maybe thousands of others just like you—a tide of humans born within forty-eight months of one another. What's more, you've probably spent most of the last decade in classrooms with a group of people born within a year of one another.

You take the same classes from the same teachers; you hear the same lectures. You read (or skim) the same textbooks, possibly along with 10,000 or 100,000 others across the country.

Of the hundreds of brands of clothing available, you wear the same five or six labels that almost everyone else wears. Of the thousands of music groups out there, your personal favorites just happen to be the favorites of a few million others your age.

You and your several million clone-peers eat the same cereals, brush with the same toothpaste (but fortunately not the same brush), visit the same stores and fast-food restaurants, watch the same TV shows, and see the same movies.

I know, I know—you're not *really* a clone. You're different from your peers in plenty of ways. But unlike any other group in society, teenagers spend the majority of their time surrounded by people who are very close in age, culture, and experience. (Imagine a company made up entirely of thirty-three- to thirty-seven-year-olds who wear Levi's.)

The problem with all this sameness is that it prevents you from reaching out to people who are different. If you want to make a difference in this world, you've got to mix it up with different people, different ages, different cultures, and different thoughts.

World Changers Talk to "Strangers"

Spending all your time with the same group of people severely limits your life. Your knowledge is limited because you have to rely on the information of people who have about the same amount of experience (or inexperience) as you have. For example, most teenagers learn about sex from peers who aren't even sure of what they're saying!

This packlike behavior also limits your fun because you're stuck only with diversions and friendships acceptable to your group. Lawn bowling and polka dances are out of the question not because they're boring—they're actually a lot of fun—but because they're socially unacceptable. Cool people don't polka; metalheads don't listen to rap; jocks don't socialize with techno-nerds.

But most important, your impact in the world is limited because your solutions show an ignorance of the big picture. If you want to shed this ignorance, you've got to step beyond the safety of your peer group and get to know some "strangers." Here are some strangers you should talk to.

Elderly People

Once upon a time in America, grandparents and older adults lived with the family. Children and teenagers spent lots of time with older people and learned about life from them. Nowadays, most people are separated from their grandparents by miles, busy lives, or death. So if you want to tap into the sixty or more years of knowledge and experience of the older generation, you've got to go out of your way to get them.

Get to know your older relatives. Let them expand your experience base by a few decades. Hear about their dreams when they were young; find out what's most important to them now. Do this before it's too late.

Other Adults

Like most humans, adults are actually kind of fun when you get to know them. The problem is, that takes time. If you don't count teachers and coaches, the amount of time each week most teenagers spend with adults can be measured in *minutes*. Maybe it's time to put adults in your schedule.

You may meet reasonably fun adults at a job or volunteer situation. Wherever you happen to find them, take the time to get to know them. Your similarities will help establish a friendship; your differences will enrich it. (Tip: you can jump start any conversation with an adult by asking, "How far did *you* have to walk in the snow to get to school?")

Kids

Back in the "good old days," families were bigger, and people tended to live closer to their relatives. You couldn't help being surrounded by kids of all shapes and sizes: brothers, sisters, nephews, nieces, cousins—and a whole bunch of other kids contributed by prolific neighbors.

Nowadays, unless you work at a day-care site or do a lot of baby-sitting, you don't spend much time with kids. Which means you're missing out on certain views of life that can be seen only through the eyes of a child. I already talked about this stuff in chapter 2, so you should already know what you're missing.

Different People

America is the great melting pot, home to people of all races, languages, religions, and classes. Yet if you're one of the 95 percent of the readers of this book who's white, middle-class, suburban, and Christian, you'll probably spend your entire life surrounded by white, middle-class, suburban, Christian people. You don't even have to *try*—it

I WAS ENCOURAGED TO ASSOCIATE WITH THOSE DIFFERENT FROM ME, BUT THIS IS BETTER THAN I COULD HAVE EXPECTED!

I'M SURE YOU MEANT TO TELL HER THAT SHE'S AS "BEAUTIFUL AS A ROBIN IN SPRING," BUT IT CAME OUT MORE LIKE "AS CREATIVE AS A PIGEON IN THE PARK."

just happens that way. You naturally seek your own people.

World changers understand this phenomenon and go out of their way to disrupt it. I encourage you to seek out and befriend people of other ethnic groups, religions, incomes, cultures, and languages. Get to know the foreign exchange students at your school, join a swim team or basketball league on the other side of town, or attend an ethnic church. But be prepared to abandon your prejudices and stereotypes—these things can't stand up to the truth.

A word of caution. I sometimes see people who've gone beyond stepping outside their peer group: they've abandoned it altogether. I see fifteen-year-olds who mix easily with adults but are social outcasts among their peers. Or black or Asian or Latino kids who despise their ethnicity.

89

World changers tear down walls that separate people—they don't leap over a wall to hide on the other side.

First learn how to relate to the people around you, then step out and get to know some strangers.

Practice Mixing It Up

Adopt a Grandparent

Go to the senior center or a nursing home in your neighborhood and tell the staff you'd like to adopt a grandparent. They'll introduce you to an older person you can spend time with one afternoon a week. The two of you can talk, play chess, read together, run errands, go hang gliding—whatever you want.

Teach Adults

Volunteer as a teacher's aide in an English as a Second Language (ESL) or other adult ed. class. Some of your teachers may moonlight as instructors in evening courses—ask around. If you help out in an ESL course, you can play tricks such as teaching them that the word for *up* is *down*, *left* is *right*, and *squirrel* is *rhinoceros*. Okay, maybe not.

Go Away

A foreign exchange program can give you a once-in-a-lifetime experience living in a foreign culture.

Stay Home

If you can't live in a foreign country, invite a foreigner to live with you. Various programs will set you up with a compatible foreign student for a period of one week to an entire year. Talk to the foreign student advisor at your school to find out how. Oh, yes, it's best to ask your parents, too.

Learn a Language

How can you reach out to people if you can't even speak their language? Forget about grades, forget about college entrance requirements—learn a second language so you can *communicate*.

MIXING WEEK

MONDAY Write a short note to a grandparent or another older relative.

TUESDAY Meet someone who's different. Take a few minutes to get to know him better.

WEDNESDAY Find someone whose native language isn't English. Ask her to teach you how to say, "Hello," "Good morning," "Please," "Thank you," and "How are you?" Take notes and practice the phrases each time you see her.

THURSDAY Interview an older person. Ask him about his dreams, great moments, favorite memories, opinions on world issues, and what he'd do differently if he had life to live over again.

FRIDAY   Hang out. Spend a half hour at the bus station, employment office, health clinic, or Social Security office. Write a short essay describing the similarities and differences between your peer group and the kinds of people you see there.

SATURDAY   Go with a friend to a sports gathering on the other side of town. Shoot hoops or play catch with some of the kids. Sit on the sidelines and talk to people around you.

SUNDAY   Go to an ethnic church—black, Latino, Korean, Chinese—whatever you can find in your area.

8

Cut It Out

Ever since you can remember, every adult from Aunt Ursula to the vice principal's secretary has told you what to do. You're dreaming of the day when they lose their right to rule you. You can't wait to be free. Just think of it! You can . . .

- stay up all night.
- eat an entire chocolate cake by yourself in your bedroom.
- cuss out your teachers.
- boss people around.
- date whoever you want, however you want.
- buy a Lamborghini and drive 200 miles an hour.

Imagine being free to do whatever you want, whenever you want: no rules, no curfews, no restrictions. If you're like most people, that isn't hard to imagine. You've been dreaming of that day ever since you were sent to your room for stuffing peas up your nose. Your mom told you to think about what you did wrong, but your three-year-old mind was busy thinking about the day when you'd be able to stuff peas up your nose whenever you felt like it.

The thought of being free to think, say, and do what you want is thrilling! So it seems a shame for me to ruin this discussion by bringing up the word *discipline*. But now that you're gaining greater freedoms in your life—and will soon graduate into many more—it's critical to understand the relationship between freedom and discipline. Here it is: *there is no freedom without discipline.*

Lots of people don't fully grasp this principle until they move out of the house for the first time. At first you think, *This is great! I can finally stay up all night, do what I want, and eat what I choose!* But when you explore the full range of these new freedoms for a few days, you develop bags under your eyes, chubby thighs, a wobbly walk, and a tendency to drool. How free are you if you have to wear a bib?

Just how free are you if you have the freedom to drink, drive, crash, and kill someone? What freedom is there if you're free to live recklessly, eat poorly, party heavily, and mess up your health, your education, and your future?

Discipline makes freedom survivable and, therefore, enjoyable. That's why people with strong discipline are the most free. They know themselves and what they're able to do, so they get the most from life.

Mind Photos

Disciplined people believe in themselves. They know their abilities. They persevere when things get tough. They say no to things that will hinder their progress. They're not afraid to cut out habits that distract them from the goal.

Of course you already know all this stuff, but there's a reason why I've stuck it in the book. If you want to make a difference in the world, you've got to develop self-discipline. And the best time to learn is *now*.

Acts of discipline are mental photographs; they provide you with evidence of your own ability. One of the best reasons to develop discipline now is to fill your brain's photo album with examples of your work.

One of my brothers is a Navy SEAL (Sea, Air, and Land commando). He jumps out of planes and helicopters and speedboats and submarines, sneaks around underwater, and blows up things—stuff like that. (He also plays a mean game of "Marco Polo," but that's beside the point.) To become a SEAL, he had to pass one of the toughest training courses in the world—less than 25 percent of those who attempt it make it through the six months of training.

People who drop out of the program are most

likely to call it quits during *hell week*. For five long days and nights, trainees are kept wet, cold, and sandy through constant swimming and exercising. They're made to run fully clothed in soft sand—carrying a telephone pole—crawl through mud flats, paddle rubber rafts twenty miles in the open ocean, and land the rafts through the surf onto rock jetties at night. And they do it all on about one hour of sleep per *day*. My brother described one of the "exercises" he endured each night, appropriately called "surf torture":

> The instructors made everyone line up on the beach, fully clothed. We linked arms, marched out into waist-deep water, and sat down. For the next ten to thirty minutes we'd sit and shiver with just our heads above water while the waves pounded us and the churned-up sand worked its way into pockets, waistbands, and socks—which we'd feel on the next run as it rubbed us raw. Sometimes, after about ten minutes, the instructors would call us out of the water. They'd let us "cool off" in the night breeze for a few minutes, then order us into the surf again.

Of course you're asking (as I did) *why?* What's the point of all the wet and cold and sand? Here's what he said:

> It's about knowing yourself and your limits. When a guy finishes *hell week*, he's had to en-

dure some pretty miserable things. But he found the self-discipline to endure the torture, so now he can look back and say, "If I made it through that, I can make it through anything." Your body will live up to the challenge if your mind decides it wants to do it.

That's the best part about discipline. When things get tough—when it seems that your goal is to change the unchangeable, beat the invincible, do the impossible—you can look back at the pictures of your past accomplishments and know that you've been to this point before and won. Every act of discipline prepares you for greater challenges ahead.

I'm not saying that discipline makes victory easy. It just makes it possible.

World Changers Are Disciplined

When you see a TV or newspaper story on someone who's making a difference in the community, all you hear about is the great things she's doing—providing food for homeless people, working with children with handicapping conditions, or starting a recycling program at school. What they don't tell you is how she got the discipline to accomplish this task.

Maybe she woke up one morning and said, "I'm going to make a difference here." Then she got up and did something about it. But if she hadn't been a person of discipline before that moment, her intentions would never have made it out of bed. Her countless acts of discipline—in study habits, health, morals, family, and spiritual matters—had prepared her for a task requiring greater discipline.

> *Your future ability to rearrange the world depends on your present ability to master your habits.*

That's why, as crazy at it seems, your future ability to rearrange the world depends on your present ability to master your habits. Each is part of the same process.

Simply Dedicated

Discipline is essential to changing the world in another way. It helps you concentrate on what's truly important. The complex distractions of our world can keep you from doing what's best. Discipline gives you the power to cut out the unnecessary stuff that saps your money, time, and attention. It gives you the strength to say no to bad and yes to good. And, more important, it helps you say no to many *good* things when they stand in the way of what's *excellent*.

Catholic nuns and priests show this kind of simple dedication when they take a vow of celibacy. They say no to lots of good things: romance, sex, honeymoons, wedding anniversaries, and children who will grow up and graduate from high school. All to say yes to one excellent thing: a life of serving God. Simple.

You don't have to be a priest or a nun to understand the value of simplicity. If you're like most students, you've got a busy and complicated life. Figure out what's most important, and learn to say no to what isn't a priority.

How to Develop Discipline

Now's the time to do it. It's kind of like the mumps—the older you get, the more it hurts. Here are discipline methods that can simplify your life and give you evidence of your ability to do even greater things.

Keep count. When I moved away to college, I began to notice how much I cussed. Nobody pointed it out to me—I just heard other people cuss a lot and realized they sounded like me. And if I sounded as stupid as they did, I knew it was time to stop.

The problem was, I couldn't. Words like *$#@*!*, *%@##!*, and even *@#$&)#$#@!!* slipped off my tongue before my mind could catch them. By the time I heard them, so did everyone else, so it was too late. It was an unconscious habit—kind of like saying *like*, like all the time . . . like you know what I, like, mean?

WOW! IS THAT A SPECIAL TALENT, OR DID YOU GO TO SCHOOL TO LEARN THAT?

To make myself more aware, I started keeping count. Each time I cussed, I'd have to take out my appointment calendar and put a mark in the corner of that day. That procedure gave me an exact count of my swears each day. It also took away my main reason for cussing: to sound cool—which is hard to do when you've let fly a brilliantly profane remark and then have to hunt through your backpack for a calendar and pen. Kind of like doing a perfect dive but losing your swimsuit in the process. It steals the thunder.

I dug out my calendar from that year—here's what happened on the first few days of counting:

Feb. 6: 6 (bad day—they canceled "Star Trek")
Feb. 7: 4
Feb. 8: 3
Feb. 9: 4
Feb. 10: 3

The tally worked. After a couple of weeks, the calendar stayed in the backpack, and I was surviving on *darn!*, *heck!*, and an occasional *shoot!* Now I have, like, other habits.

Gang up on it. For lots of people, putting down others is a serious habit. In some friendship circles it's the primary form of communicating. But it's tough to stop shooting put-downs if your close friends continue to launch them at you. So call a cease-fire. For one week, no put-downs: no name calling, no insults, no criticism, no sarcasm. If you get caught in the act, you get punched in the arm.

A few days—and two sore arms—later, you'll feel like a fog has lifted from your friendships. If you're pleased with the results, continue it for another week. This time put-downers pay for their cuts with sodas.

You can use this kind of collective discipline for any behavior, good or bad, as long as you can find at least one other person to work on it with you. Set up rewards and consequences to encourage you along the way.

Tell someone. I feel funny writing about the virtues of discipline right now—this book was due last month and I'm still typing. A few of my friends know I'm behind, so every few days they call to encourage me. On a day like today, when it's sunny and the waves look good (okay, so I peeked), they call me a lot. Their gentle push helps to keep me writing. (Now if the phone would just stop ringing, I might get some work done.)

If you're trying to develop discipline in a tough area of your life, tell someone. His or her encouragement and gentle prodding can ease the journey.

Push your limit. I've always thought of myself as a big-time meat eater. Hot pastrami sandwiches, sausage, barbecued chicken, Lebanon bologna, charbroiled hamburgers, BLT's, and ground beef tacos—these are a few of my favorite things. So when a vegetarian friend asked me to try going without meat for a while, I laughed. No way—I'd starve.

But after I thought about it, I realized it would be an interesting challenge. I could try it for a month just to prove to myself that I could conquer my craving for meat through careful discipline. I never went back to eating meat. That was thirteen years ago. I still miss the pastrami sandwiches.

Take something you "can't live without" and cut it out for a time. Use the exercise to strengthen your willpower and remind you of who's in control. It makes a great mind photo for later challenges.

IT'S OK., DAD, I'M GIVING UP HOMEWORK FOR A WHILE AS A PART OF LEARNING DISCIPLINE.

One day at a time. Some disciplines are just too big to conquer all at once. Making a decision to quit for all time is too much to handle. That's why Alcoholics Anonymous and other groups that help people with dependencies encourage you to take it "one day at a time." You can handle just about *anything* for one day. The next day, it's the same thing—there's no need to worry about next week, next month, next year. You just have to make it today.

If you're caught in an addictive behavior that's starting to control you, stop doing it today. When you wake up tomorrow, say the same thing. Addictive behaviors are tough to beat, but you can do it one day at a time.

Ask for help. If you have a drug or an alcohol dependency or you're dealing with some other compulsive behavior such as overeating or purging, you're going to need more than discipline and willpower to overcome it. Usually the behavior is a symptom of a deeper problem. That doesn't mean you can't beat it—it's just going to take some help.

I know you've heard this speech a hundred times in school, but in case you ditched class a lot, here it is again. Talk to a teacher, counselor, pastor, or youth leader. A trusted adult can connect you with someone who'll help with the behavior problem and also help you clean out some of the guilt or anger or depression that you might have hidden inside. Life is tough, but it doesn't have to be *that* tough.

A Final Thought on Discipline

I'm afraid some people reading this chapter will feel horribly guilty about how undisciplined they are compared to my examples. To assuage (cool word, huh?) their guilt, they'll count their cussing, stop their put-downs, give up meat, write a book, feed the homeless, enter a convent, and become Navy SEALs. This week.

If you're one of those people, I have two words to say to you: "Back off!"

Discipline is not a competitive sport. Comparing yourself to these examples—or anyone else's—won't make you more disciplined. I have a friend who prays two hours a *day*. My brother can swim ten miles in the ocean—at night. I know a guy who runs six miles at lunch each day. I know people who read a book a week. *And* write a letter a day.

If I insist on comparing myself to them, I'll always be an undisciplined failure. On the other hand, I don't have to look far to find people who *never* exercise or pray or read or write. In comparison to them, I'm a pillar of discipline.

In discipline, your only true competition is yourself. If you want to make a difference in the world, you've got to beat the voice inside that says, "You can't do it—give up." Every act of discipline now is a self-portrait—a picture of you winning.

DISCIPLINE WEEK

Practice small acts of discipline this week. Take on these challenges each day to give you small photos of what you can accomplish.

MONDAY No TV today.

TUESDAY Say yes—no yeahs or uh-huhs.

WEDNESDAY No put-downs.

THURSDAY Do one hundred sit-ups any way you want to do them.

FRIDAY No meat today—and for the next six days!

SATURDAY Wake up at five; walk for one hour; make breakfast for your family.

SUNDAY Memorize Proverbs 2, the first five verses.

9

Give It Away

Life starts out so simple. You show up naked, dimpled, tiny. But within moments, they're piling possessions on you: a name, a diaper, clothes, toys—and one of those mobiles that hangs over your crib, just out of reach, driving you absolutely crazy.

It doesn't stop there. Your life becomes an endless consumption of *stuff*—new clothes to replace the ones you grow out of, new toys to replace the ones you broke, lost, or ate. Then it's trikes and bikes, books and tapes, and still more clothes. By the time you're a teenager, you're a full-time consumer: shoes, clothes, jewelry, CDs, tapes, videos, stereos, phones, TVs, VCRs, computers, mountain bikes, skateboards, skis, cars. And you're still just getting started; you'll be acquiring stuff for the next sixty years.

I'm sure you've seen the bumper sticker, "He who dies with the most toys wins." It's a silly idea, yet lots of people live as if they believe it. Cheering you on are the countless commercials showing you what you'll need to buy to "win." Commercials make up about 20 percent of television programming. The average teenager watches twenty hours of television a week. So by the time you're eighteen, you've seen about 350,000 commercials. No wonder you can't get those stupid jingles out of your head.

Even if you don't watch TV, you're still getting

hit over the head with advertising: on the radio, in magazines and movie theaters, on buses, benches, billboards, and the back of your cereal box.

The ads are working. Teenagers are spending more money (theirs and their parents') on "stuff" than ever before. For example, 50 percent have their own TV; 44 percent own a VCR; 33 percent of those aged sixteen and older own a car. Teenage girls spend over $5 billion annually on cosmetics, $16 billion on clothes.

In 1989 alone, you and your twenty-three million friends spent over $71 *billion*. The big question is, *What are you getting for your money?* Not peace: the number of suicides, homicides, and cases of depression keeps increasing despite all the toys that should make life more pleasant. Not fulfillment: no matter how much you buy, how many clothes in your closet, how fast your car goes, you cannot fill the emptiness inside you.

World Changers Are Big Givers

The bumper sticker would be correct if it read, "He who *tries* for the most toys loses." I think the only way to win the race is to run *backward*. Instead of trying to collect wealth, try to give it away.

Give Money

"Wait a minute! I don't have enough money to afford giving some of it away," you say. I beg to differ. Almost all of your parents' income has to go toward rent, utilities, taxes, insurance, food, medical bills, and your clothes. You, however, can spend most of your money any way you please.

Sure, you spend lots of your money on food and clothes, but you wouldn't starve or go naked if you didn't—the closet and refrigerator at your house are subsidized by your folks. Unlike them, you spend most of your money on wants, not needs. Compared to most adults, you're rich. Which means you're able to give away a greater percentage of your income.

GIVE AWAY MY MONEY !!!?!

Sometimes you see TV preachers who say that if you're "faithful" and give money (to them, it's assumed), God will make you wealthy. I think this is a stupid idea. One of the best reasons to give money is to help *other* people, but these guys turn the act of giving into a selfish thing. I think if that's the motive, it's better to just keep the money and leave God out of it.

FRIENDS, THE LAWD HAS TOLD ME THAT HE WANTS YOU TO SEND YOUR MONEY TO ME.. ... IN FAITH.

Giving to a worthy cause *does* have its rewards. You feel that you're doing something to change the world—which is a wonderful feeling. If you give regularly, you sense a feeling of accomplishment— it takes discipline to do this. And when you give to a cause, you have more authority to speak out on it—you're now an *investor* in change. (I don't have much respect for people who complain about hunger or homelessness or the environment yet won't give their time or money to change the situation. It's put up or shut up.)

In one way, those "prosperity preachers" are right. Giving can make you richer because in order to give regularly, you have to learn to manage your money. And the better you handle your money, the more you'll save. For example, if you don't have any obligation to give, you can spend freely on CDs and food and movie tickets. But if someone is counting on the $30 you give every month, you're going to think twice about blowing your paycheck on "stuff."

Give smart. Lots of people and organizations would like for you to give your money to them. Unfortunately, some of them are crooks. The crooked ones not only "steal" your money. They also steal your desire to give, so legitimate causes lose out because you fear you can't trust anyone. When you give money, it's *your* responsibility to know where that money is going. Ask questions.

Is it a nonprofit organization? If an organization is authorized by the government to accept tax-deductible donations, it's called a 501(c)(3) corporation, which refers to the paragraph in some tax code that explains this. That doesn't automatically make it legitimate, but you know it has to follow certain rules that make ripping you off more difficult.

What percentage of your money goes toward "the cause"? Like any corporation, nonprofits have to pay rent, utilities, phone bills, postage, salaries, and so on. Some also have large advertising costs— TV ads, brochures, and mailings. Most respected organizations are able to put at least 80¢ of every dollar into the cause.

Warning: beware telephone fund-raisers. Crooked or questionable organizations often call and announce they represent such-and-such association, a name that sounds an awful lot like the name of a legitimate organization but isn't. Those who do lots of telephone soliciting often pay a for-profit company to do the calling—and give it a percentage of every dollar they collect. If you're interested in giving, don't pledge on the phone. Instead, tell the person to send you some literature that explains where the money will go, in what percentage, and so on. If he's legitimate, he'll understand. If he's crooked or being paid a commission on every telephone pledge, he won't like your idea at all. In that case, say good-bye.

Give every month. The best way to give is to donate a set amount each month to one or more organizations. That way, they can count on your money month after month (imagine an employer who paid you "whenever she felt like it"). It's also easier for you to budget your giving. Treat it like any other monthly expense such as rent or a car payment. The difference is that this is a payment you *want* to make.

Lots of people give a percentage of their income—5 percent, 10 percent, 20 percent, 40 percent. At the end of the month you add up all your income, figure out the portion that you will give away, then write the checks. If you made lots of money and have some gift money left after making your regular contributions, give a one-time gift to a special cause.

I believe the simplest and most effective monthly gift is to support a needy child. I cannot think of a better use for your money than to provide food, education, and hope for a kid in another part of the world. For about $21 a month, *you* can change the world for one other person. That's two cassettes or four movies or five trips to McDonald's. For lots of kids, $21 is a big sacrifice. Is it too much to pay to save the life of a child? Give it away. If you're interested in child sponsorship, contact Compassion International, P.O. Box 7000, Colorado Springs, CO 80933, 719-594-9900.

Give up. The best part of percentage giving is upping the percentage each year! Chances are, your income has increased, so you can give an extra percentage point and still have money left over. Let's say you start with a commitment to give 5 percent of your income each month. After the first year (or six months, if you're gutsy), raise the commitment to 6 percent. Or if you start at 10 percent (much better), graduate to 11 percent. The goal is to keep doing this each year.

I know what you're thinking: *If I do this every year, by the time I'm sixty I'll be giving away over* half *my income every month!* Yes! That's the point. You can't even begin to imagine the impact you'll have on this world by investing so heavily into changing it.

Give Stuff

The first time I moved away from home, my worldly possessions fit into a backpack and a couple of duffle bags. At the next move I had added a

119

couple of cardboard boxes of stuff to the baggage. By the time I moved again, I filled a VW van with junk acquired since my last migration. Now when I move, I need a twenty-foot U-Haul truck and three buff friends to help me load it—and I can't even *find* my backpack.

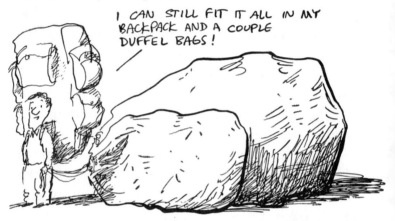

I CAN STILL FIT IT ALL IN MY BACKPACK AND A COUPLE DUFFEL BAGS!

How did my life get filled with so much stuff? Then I remember: I brought it in myself. Not all at once—I would have noticed such shameless materialism. I acquired it one piece at a time.

A lot of the things I have are necessities: my toothbrush, sleeping bag, and Spiderman pj's. Some of my possessions are *almost* essential: my Craftsman socket wrench set and pink polyester tuxedo. But most of the stuff is pure luxury—bicycles, surfboards, stereos, backpacking gear, and enough clothes to outfit a family of twenty-seven.

Lately I've been thinking that I don't need all

this stuff. I don't need the clutter. I don't need the headaches and expenses of fixing and mending—something is always breaking. I don't need the worry of its being stolen. So I've begun a nonaccumulation policy.

Here's how it works. Whenever I want to get something new, I have to get rid of something like it. If I want a new shirt, I go to my closet and pick out a shirt to give away. A pair of new shoes costs me one pair of old shoes given to Goodwill. Christmas is the toughest because I get lots of clothes as gifts and have to give away as many items.

Okay, so there are a few things I *don't* do this with. Socks and underwear, for example. Fourteen pairs of underwear mean I can go two weeks without doing laundry. My goal is sixty pairs. I also don't give away books, which are an investment I can use again and again in my writing. At least that's the excuse I use when I'm at the bookstore.

The biggest problem with the nonaccumulation policy is that I hate to give away things that mean a lot to me—an old baseball glove, an address book, my first baggy swim trunks. I put these things in a keepsakes box where they stay exempt from the rule. (Now if I can just figure out how to fit my old VW van into that box . . .)

No more piles. Why not adopt a nonaccumulation policy in your life? Start by pulling out of your closet, dressers, and shelves all the stuff that's just taking up space. Box it up and take it to the Salvation Army, Goodwill, or some other agency that can use your old clothes and toys. Warning: since your parents probably bought you a lot of this stuff, it's wise to let them look through the pile before you give it away.

Now abide by the rule. If you want a new pair of pants, pick out the pair it will replace. A new toy? What will you swap for it? After a while, your buying habits will change—getting a new toy will cost you money, and it'll cost you an old toy you like as much.

The best part about this policy is that it compels you to attach the act of *receiving* to the act of *giving*. If you *want* something, you must *give* something. And the people you give it to will appreciate it.

Merry Christmas

I think one of the reasons why Christmas is the biggest holiday is that it is the one time of the year when virtually everyone, regardless of religion, *gives*. It's not people's wallets and checkbooks that do the giving—it's their hearts. And when they do, it changes them.

The sad thing is, many people wait until December to do what their hearts would have them do all year if they stopped to listen. World changers listen to their hearts. They give away their time and money and possessions to people and causes they care about—all year long. In a way, they make every month December and every day Christmas. Pass the eggnog.

GIVING WEEK

MONDAY   Hide twenty nickels in your little brother's pants—don't tell him you did it.

TUESDAY   Slip $2 in coins through the slots of a friend's locker.

WEDNESDAY Give $5 to a total stranger.

GEE, I'D <u>LIKE</u> TO DO THIS "GIVING WEEK" THING... BUT I NEED TO GIVE <u>MYSELF</u> SOMETHING, TOO... LIKE A NEW STEREO SYSTEM, NEW SKATEBOARD, NEW CLOTHES, NEW.......

THURSDAY   Do a monthly budget to figure out how much money you earn and what you spend it on. Decide to give away a percentage.

FRIDAY   Fill out the form in the back of this book and send it to Compassion International to find out about sponsoring a child.

SATURDAY   Begin a nonaccumulation policy. Give away the stuff you don't need.

SUNDAY   Give an hour of your day to someone who could use it. Run an errand for a neighbor, mow the lawn for someone, clean out the garage, scrub the kitchen floor, or pick up trash at a park.

10
Walk Upside Down

If you've read all the chapters so far, you've probably realized that each one takes a piece of conventional wisdom and turns it on its head.

Conventional Wisdom	Upside-Down Wisdom
Get serious.	Dream big.
Grow up.	Be a child.
Sit still.	Stand.
Do as you're told.	Question authority.
Go for the grades.	Think again.
Be number one.	Be last.

Don't talk to strangers.	Mix it up.
If it feels good, do it.	Cut it out.
Buy now.	Give it away.

In other words, to make a difference, a world changer has to look at life upside down. Which is where we started this whole thing in chapter 1. (If you're *still* lying down, maybe it's time to get up now.)

Upside-down wisdom makes sense when you realize the mess we've made of this world by following the right-side-up kind. In every chapter so far, I've asked you to chuck the conventional way of doing things and walk upside down instead.

I tried to be careful about which conventional wisdom I told you to reject. For example, conven-

tional wisdom tells us that it's not good to play freeze tag on the freeway. I think that's a pretty good rule, so I didn't include a chapter, "Hide in the Center Divider." There are a few other pieces of conventional wisdom that I believe ought to remain right side up:

- Buckle up.
- Look both ways.
- Beware of dog.
- Don't spit into the wind.
- Two prunes are enough.

So how did I decide which ones to flip upside down? I studied the lives of people who've made a difference and discovered that many of them have flipped the same pieces of conventional wisdom.

World Changers Walk Upside Down

What gives me the confidence to print these pieces of upside-down wisdom in a book is that I also found each of them by studying the life of Jesus—and I believe He is the greatest world changer who ever lived.

Although lots of people think of Jesus as the tall, dark, glassy-eyed man seen hugging sheep in those pictures in Sunday school class, He was really a radical. Many of His ideas were so crazy that people thought He was a religious basket case. Others thought He was demon possessed. Some thought He was just a troublemaker trying to overthrow the government.

But a few thought He was God, so they wrote down the wild things He said and did and tried to live according to His upside-down wisdom. When you read about this Jesus, you see how He turned conventional wisdom on its head.

For example, when some people were arguing about who was the greatest, Jesus said, "If anyone desires to be first, he shall be last of all and servant of all." That's where I got the idea for chapter 6, "Be Last."

Another time He was talking to a crowd, and some kids tried to get up close to Him. The adults thought the kids were being pests so they kept the kids away. But Jesus said to let them through! He grabbed one of the kids and said to the adults, "Unless you . . . become as little children, you will by no means enter the kingdom of heaven." You can bet that shut the adults up. That is why I wrote chapter 2, "Be a Child."

Jesus wasn't afraid to stand for what was right. One day He went to the temple in Jerusalem and saw the courtyard filled with merchants buying and selling stuff—kind of like a swap meet. He got ticked and started flipping over tables and chasing the people away! He told them that they'd taken a house of prayer and turned it into a robbers' den. He asked the question, "What's wrong with this picture?"—then He did something about it. Hence, chapter 3, "Stand."

I THOUGHT HE WAS SUPPOSED TO BE SOME "MEEK & MILD" TYPE!

He told people to question the authority of the religious teachers whose rules were unfair and whose lives were filled with hypocrisy. He encouraged people to give to God not just a portion of their possessions but *everything*. Jesus told them to develop self-discipline rather than rely on the arbitrary rules imposed by others. He showed them that true wisdom shows up in your heart, not just in your head (or your report card).

Here is His most radical teaching: "Greater love has no one than this, than to lay down one's life for his friends." Then He did exactly that. This one act of supreme sacrifice completely rearranged the world. He gave each of us the opportunity to make a difference in the world by serving the One who created it.

If you want to become a world changer, study people who've changed the world. If you want to see what the world could become with your help, study the One who created it.

Study the life of Jesus, and you'll do both.

UPSIDE-DOWN WEEK

Read these stories from Jesus' life, and catch a glimpse of how He turned the world's wisdom upside down.

MONDAY   *Be a child*. The price of being too grown up: Matthew 18:2–5 (which means book of Matthew, chapter 18, verses 2 through 5).

TUESDAY   *Stand*. Jesus makes a mess: Mark 11:15–18.

WEDNESDAY *Question authority*. Jesus grades the teachers: Luke 11:37–54.

THURSDAY   *Be last*. Jesus the foot washer: John 13:1–17.

FRIDAY   *Mix it up.* Jesus befriends the "other" people: Luke 5:12–13; 14:12–14; 19:1–10.

SATURDAY   *Give it away.* Jesus shows the true value of "stuff": Luke 12:13–21.

SUNDAY   *Walk upside down.* Jesus flips conventional wisdom on its head: Luke 6:20–26.

APPENDIX

Four Needs
for
Right Now

1

AIDS

When AIDS first caught the attention of the American people back in the early eighties, most of us thought, *What a tragedy for all those gay men and drug addicts, but that's what happens when you do those kinds of things.* It's taken a few years, but the truth is starting to sink in: AIDS isn't a gay problem or a druggie problem. It's everybody's problem.

According to the World Health Organization, 30 million adults and 10 million children worldwide will be infected with the AIDS virus by the year 2000.[1] That's 40 *million* people—that's equivalent to the entire population of Canada and Australia combined.

Here in the U.S., over 100,000 people are known to have died from the disease. The Centers for Disease Control figures that as many as 30 per-

1. Reported in *U.S. News & World Report*, May 13, 1991, p. 17.

cent of AIDS deaths are never reported as such, out of shame and misdiagnosis.

As of this writing, 170,000 people *know* they have AIDS. Some researchers estimate that the number of people carrying the virus—who know it or not—is around 1 million. And unless we come up with a cure, they'll all die from it.

JUST LOOK AT THAT MAN! LOOK HOW HE WALKS! SEE THE CLOTHES HE'S WEARING! I'LL BET HE'S GAY, HAS AIDS, AND IS INFECTING EVERYONE HE KNOWS! WHAT A SLIME!

YOU'RE MISSING YOUR GLASSES. THAT'S YOUR HUSBAND.

The AIDS epidemic is tragic, but it's not hopeless. Here's what you can do to help.

Protect Yourself

The first thing you can do about AIDS is to protect yourself. The safest way to do this as a teenager is to postpone having sex. The virus can hide in a person's body for up to ten years without being detected. So when you have sex with someone, it's as if you're having sex with everyone your partner has had sex with in the past decade (and everyone *that person* had sex with and so on). If any of those people carried the virus, you can get it. Add to this the risk of picking up other sexually transmitted diseases, the possibility of pregnancy, and all the emotional effects of early sexual experiences, and you have to ask yourself, Is it really worth it?

If you do have sex, use a condom. No other birth control device offers that kind of protection. In one survey, 70 percent of the teenagers questioned believed that birth control pills can prevent AIDS. Wrong.

The virus hops from one body to another through semen, vaginal fluid, and blood. You can get the virus if any of these fluids from an infected person make it into your own bloodstream. These fluids can get to your blood through a woman's uterus or through tiny abrasions and sores on your genitals. The friction of body parts rubbing together is enough to form such an abrasion. That's one of the reasons gay men have been so susceptible to AIDS—anal sex causes more abrasions.

You can get AIDS through oral sex—semen or vaginal fluids can get to your bloodstream via the stomach or throat. An infected person's saliva rarely contains the virus, but if there's blood in it—say, from cutting a tongue on braces—you can be exposed.

For more information on how you can prevent the spreading of AIDS, contact:

AIDS Information Ministries
P.O. Box 136116

Fort Worth, TX 76136
(817) 237-0230

They have brochures and a great video you can use to teach AIDS prevention. These people also hold assemblies and seminars nationwide. If you think your school or youth group needs to know more about AIDS, talk to them about doing a presentation for you.

Comfort People with AIDS

Many individuals with AIDS are treated like lepers—people don't want to touch them, comfort them, or even see them. Many otherwise compassionate people are hesitant to get involved with anyone with AIDS for fear of contracting the disease themselves.

The risk is much smaller than many people realize. Unlike a cold or a flu bug, the AIDS virus is actually very fragile, dying within seconds of exposure to the air. You need to take the same basic sanitary precautions you'd use with any sick person: avoid body fluids and open wounds. Of the tens of thousands of families that have a person with AIDS living at home, not one has reported another family member becoming infected through normal contact. (Exceptions are mothers who've passed the virus to their unborn children and spouses who've been infected through sex.)

You can make a big difference in the life of a person with AIDS just by becoming a friend. Doing this is going to take initiative: call your county health department, local churches, or local hospitals to see if they provide services to persons with AIDS.

Most people with AIDS aren't hospitalized or even bedridden. But because the virus is destroying their immune system, they're often sick and can't exert themselves very much. Here are some of the ways you can volunteer:

141

- If you have a car, you can provide transportation to the doctor or to a grocery store.
- You can do errands for people who are too sick to leave the house. Mow the law; clean the house; do the ironing.
- You can just visit with the person—talk, laugh, be a friend.
- Some children have AIDS. You can play with them, read stories together, or be a baby-sitter.

It's okay to team up with a friend or two on this. Pick an afternoon each week when you and your friend volunteer to help those with AIDS.

2
Disasters

War in the Persian Gulf, drought in Ethiopia, a cyclone in Bangladesh—political and natural disasters requiring international relief strike somewhere on the globe every two to three weeks. Here in the U.S. tens of thousands of people each year have their homes and lives rearranged by floods, tornadoes, hurricanes, earthquakes, fires, and accidents.

Survivors of these disasters worldwide can count on one thing: the Red Cross will be there to help. The American and International Red Cross come to the aid of those in need, regardless of race, religion, or politics. They do their amazing work through volunteers like you.

If you want to make a difference for the victims of disaster, here's how to start. Look in the phone book for the number of your local American Red Cross chapter and ask for the Office of Volunteers or the Health and Safety Department. Tell them you want to help. Here are a few of the ways they might be able to use you.

Host a Blood Drive

Through drives set up by people like you, the Red Cross gathers more than half the nation's blood supply. Because blood has a shelf life of about six weeks, the Red Cross is always looking for donors. You can organize a blood drive for your school, church, sports league, or—if you have a big family—next reunion. You will be helping supply something that almost all people will need in their lifetimes.

Collect Cash

Raise money to help the victims of a recent disaster. Because of news coverage, people will already know about the need. What they want is assurance that their contribution will go where it's intended—to the people who need it. When donors know that you're raising money on behalf of the Red Cross, they know it will be used properly.

Take a Course

Get some friends together and take courses through your local chapter. Your knowledge of CPR, first aid, and water safety can help avert a disaster among your family and friends. What's more fulfilling than saving a human life?

145

Join the Club

Many chapters of the American Red Cross have complete disaster preparedness clubs for young people. Members of Youth Disaster Action Teams (YDAT) and Youth in Emergency Services (YiES) join with other students in their area to take courses in first aid, CPR, crisis intervention, earthquake preparedness, and damage assessment. Programs vary from area to area (e.g., earthquakes are a big topic in California chapters). But no matter where you live, someday disaster will strike. Membership in one of these programs will prepare you for that day.

Be a Counselor

Some Red Cross chapters have a program called the Peer Assistance League (PAL). When you join a PAL, you take a peer counseling course that will enable you to help other teenagers cope with a personal disaster such as depression, a drug problem, or a family crisis.

By the way, other organizations in your community may sponsor peer counseling courses—your school counselor can tell you whom to contact.

3

Environment

In science fiction books and films, one theme predominates: life on other planets. It's an intriguing thought—if we succeed in making this planet uninhabitable, we can move to a new one. But that's why it's called science *fiction*. The science *fact*—as of this writing, anyway— is that no other planets will suit us humans. We're stuck with what we've got.

That's a sobering thought considering how fast we're destroying it. We've made a big mess of the land, air, and water. If you want to help stop the destruction, you've got to help clean up the mess.

You can take many actions to reduce your household's consumption of resources and to make your community kinder to the planet. The most helpful resource I've ever seen on this is the book *50 Simple Things You Can Do to Save the Earth* by the Earthworks Group. The book's title says it all—pick up a copy and start making a difference. Until you can make it to the bookstore, here are just a few ideas to get you started.

Recycle

We're running out of places to bury our trash. The shame is that much of what gets buried can be recycled instead. To set up a trash sorting center for your household, clear out a space in a closet or the garage to store your recyclables. Next, label a set of boxes: one each for aluminum cans, plastic bottles, clear glass, colored glass, and paper. Leave room next to the boxes for your newspaper stack. Now get your family to use them!

You'll have to find a recycling center nearby. Depending on the size of your boxes and the eating habits of your family, you'll need to make trips there every couple of weeks or so.

Be sure to rinse out the containers and remove the caps and tops before you box them. You can leave the labels on—they'll be burned off during recycling. Some recycling centers take household paper as well as newspaper. If yours does, recycle your magazines, junk mail, cereal boxes, and notebook and computer paper. I keep a brown paper bag beside my desk. Instead of throwing these types of paper in the trash, I file them in the bag. When the bag is full, I carry it out to my sorting area.

Make a Pile

Recycle your kitchen and garden leftovers into topsoil for the yard. Fence in a composting area with chicken wire and wooden stakes. The area should be about two feet deep, three to four feet wide, and two feet tall. You can make it smaller or larger to fit your space. Toss in grass cuttings, leaves, garden cuttings, and any organic garbage from your kitchen—the things you usually stuff down the garbage disposal or throw in the trash. Cover up food scraps in the pile to keep critters away from them. Another thing: a compost pile is happier as a vegetarian, so don't feed it meat, bones, or fat.

In a couple of months nature will have turned your garbage into hearty soil that any plant would love to dig its roots into. By the way, serious composters have two or three piles going at a time so that one is always ready to be returned to the garden. You can learn more on composting by reading a gardening book or asking someone at your local nursery.

Don't Buy It

Lots of packages can't be recycled easily. If you keep buying them, the manufacturers will keep making them, and the landfills will keep trying to swallow them. So shop wisely. You can affect what they make by buying only those products that can be recycled.

Hand It Down

I talked about this in chapter 9, "Give It Away." If you have clothing, toys, sports equipment, or furniture that you don't want, give it to someone who will. Your discards will have a new life with someone else—and you'll postpone the need for more landfill space.

Use the Off Switch

Make a habit of turning off lights, stereos, TVs, and anything else you're not using at the moment. The less electricity you use, the less fuel the power plant has to burn, and the air gets a little bit cleaner.

Do the same with the heater. Turn it off at night when you're cozy in your bed; the rest of the time just turn it down and wear a sweater.

WHY DON'T WE JUST TURN OFF THE LIGHTS AND SAVE ENERGY?

WHY DON'T WE JUST TURN YOU OFF? WE'LL SAVE A WHOLE LOT MORE!

Pick Up Trash

Form a work crew of your friends and go out to pick up trash. Arm yourselves with a box of large trash bags and comb a beach, park, or field for litter. Carry two bags each—one for recyclables and one for plain old ugly trash. Be sure to wear gloves, too. When you're finished, sort the recyclables into glass, aluminum, and plastic drink containers. To make things fun, see who can fill the most bags and who can find the most unusual piece of litter. When you're through picking and sorting, have a picnic in your beautified spot.

Save at School

Think about the resources used up every day at your school: electricity, paper, water, food, and containers. Get students to conserve and recycle these things.

- Ask the food service to stop selling food in Styrofoam containers.
- Set up collection barrels for aluminum cans.
- Place boxes in classrooms where notebook and computer paper can be stacked for recycling.
- Ask someone to fix the shower that's been leaking ever since your father graduated from the school.

4

Homeless People

Trevor Farrell was eleven years old when he saw a news story on homeless people in his city. People living in the street. Living in boxes. Huddled on curbsides. Digging in trash cans for food. He couldn't believe it. People living like that in his own city! He had to do something.

He grabbed a blanket from the closet and talked his dad into driving him downtown. Seeing a man on the sidewalk in the cold, he got out of the car and wrapped the blanket around the man's shoulders. He turned back to his dad's station wagon and went home. The next day he took a few more blankets and did the same for some other people.

After that, he took blankets and food. It went on nightly. Friends joined in, and soon that one night's urge to do something had blossomed into a full-blown operation—an organization with a homeless shelter, a thrift store, and hundreds of local volunteers serving meals to the homeless.

In the U.S. over three million people have no home. There are dozens of reasons why they don't. Many are mental patients who've fallen through the cracks of an overburdened mental health system. Some are drug addicts down on their luck. Others are just out of a job, out of money, and out of touch with family and friends who could help them. The saddest ones are women and children who've had to flee an abusive home. And a few are just lazy bums.

Regardless of how they ended up on the streets, they're there. And they can use your help. For practical ideas on what you can do to make a difference, pick up a copy of *52 Ways to Help Homeless People* by Gray Temple, Jr. (we're not related), published in 1991 by Oliver-Nelson Books. Here are some ideas you can start with right now.

Buy a Burrito

Next time you go into a fast-food restaurant and see a homeless person outside, buy an extra portion of food and give it to him. You won't have to worry about whether your money is going to buy drugs or alcohol—you know it's buying him a meal.

Collect Clothing

Have members of your family go through their closets and drawers to pick out what they're willing to give away. Bag it all up and take it to a homeless shelter or some other agency that works with people on the streets.

Build a House

Habitat for Humanity is an organization that specializes in building houses for poor people around the world. Here in the U.S., it organizes teams of volunteers (like yourself) to help build houses for people who couldn't otherwise afford them. Local chapters are all over the country, including student chapters on school campuses. To find out how to get involved with Habitat in your area, contact the national office:

Habitat for Humanity
121 Habitat Street
Americus, GA 31709-3498
(912) 924-6935

Hold a "Comic Relief"

HBO puts on a show called "Comic Relief" to raise money for homeless people, using humor and drama to spotlight the problem of homelessness in America. Why not get your school or club to host one of its own? You may not be able to get Whoopi Goldberg or Robin Williams to show up, but you can ask some of your funnier friends to help you put something together. Sell tickets and give the proceeds to an agency working with homeless people in your area.

Give Your Time

Why not volunteer at a shelter, rescue mission, or soup kitchen? These facilities are usually run by churches or other nonprofit organizations, so they're always needing volunteers to talk to people, cook and serve food, clean up, and do lots of other jobs.

STUFF ABOUT THE AUTHOR

Todd Temple is the cofounder and executive director of 10 TO 20, a company that produces national events and conferences designed to get students involved in making a difference. He's written or cowritten nine books, including *Creative Dating* (a reasonably funny book celebrating the notion that there's more to dating than dinner and a movie) and *How to Become a Teenage Millionaire* (which actually is all about how to make, save, and spend money wisely). He's also a semi-regular contributor to teenage magazines and a motivational speaker to students at schools, churches, and conferences.

Todd holds a bachelor's degree in social ecology from the University of California, Irvine. His interests include literature, computers, theater, surfing, bicycling, travel, and hunger relief. He lives in Del Mar, California.